Step by Step

The Story of a Frog

It Starts with a Tadpole

Shannon Zemlicka

Lerner Publications ◆ Minneapolis

Lerner Publications Company
An imprint of Lerner Publishing Group, Inc.
241 First Avenue North
Minneapolis, MN 55401 USA

For reading levels and more information, look up this title at www.lernerbooks.com.

Image credits: Kurit Afsheen/EyeEm/Getty Images, p. 3; Jake Booth/EyeEm/Getty Images, pp. 4–5, 23 (top left); Adrian Bosio/EyeEm/Getty Images, pp. 6–7, 23 (bottom left); mauribo/iStock/Getty Images, pp. 8–9, 23 (bottom right); Suwat wongkham/Shutterstock.com, pp. 10–11; Wild Horizons/Universal Images/Getty Images, pp. 12–13;Steve Byland/Shutterstock.com, pp. 14–15, 23 (top right); ePhotocorp/iStock/Getty Images, pp. 16–17; Matt Meadows/Photolibrary/Getty Images, pp. 18–19; kororokerokero/Getty Images, pp. 20–21; BrianLasenby/iStock/Getty Images, p. 22. Cover: Jennifer Shields/jjs08 images/Getty Images (tadpoles); GlobalP/iStock/Getty Images (frog).

Main body text set in Mikado a Medium.
Typeface provided by HVD Fonts.

Library of Congress Cataloging-in-Publication Data

The Cataloging-in-Publication Data for *The Story of a Frog: It Starts with a Tadpole* is on file at the Library of Congress.
ISBN 978-1-5415-9724-2 (lib. bdg.)
ISBN 978-1-72841-434-8 (pbk.)
ISBN 978-1-72840-108-9 (eb pdf)

Manufactured in the United States of America
1-47828-48268-10/4/2019

Ribbit!

Here is a frog.
How does a frog grow?

Tiny tadpoles grow.

A tadpole
leaves its egg.

Its tail gets longer.

The tadpole
starts to swim.

The tadpole
starts to eat.

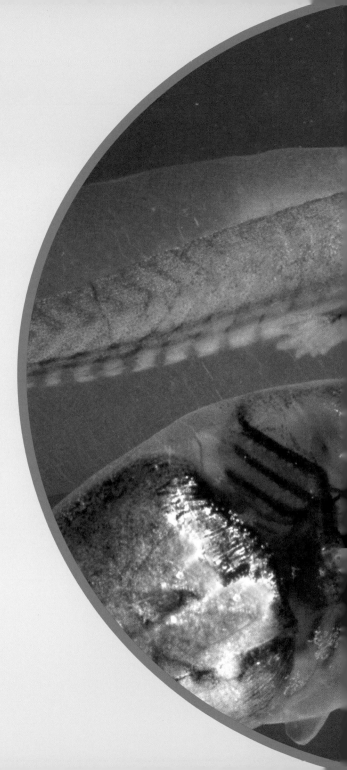

Back legs grow.

Front legs grow.

The tadpole leaves
the water.

Its tail shrinks.

Hello, frog!

Picture Glossary

egg

legs

tadpole

tail

Read More

Hurley, Jorey. *Ribbit*. New York: Simon & Schuster Books for Young Readers, 2017.

Kenan, Tessa. *It's a Red-Eyed Tree Frog!* Minneapolis: Lerner Publications, 2017.

Vasilyeva, Anastasiya. *Frog*. New York: Bearport, 2017.

Index